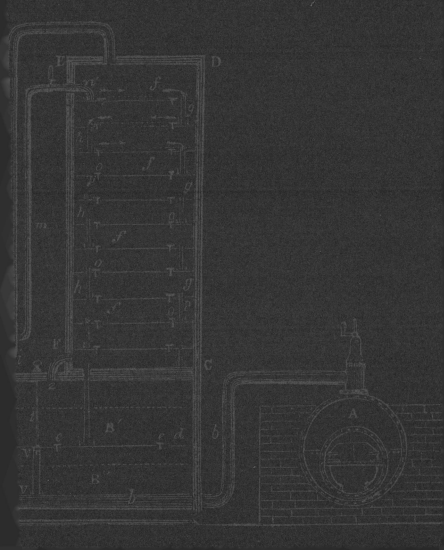

THE PHILOSOPHY OF
GIN

THE PHILOSOPHY OF
GIN

JANE PEYTON

First published 2020 by
The British Library
96 Euston Road
London NW1 2DB

ISBN 978 0 7123 5360 1
eISBN 978 0 7123 6781 3
Cataloguing in Publication Data
A catalogue record for this book is available
from the British Library

Designed and typeset by Sandra Friesen
Printed and bound in the Czech Republic by Finidr

MIX
Paper | Supporting
responsible forestry
FSC® C014138

CONTENTS

GINTRODUCTION

GIN IS IN; of that there is no doubt. Just look at the glass wall of bottles in shops and bars, with a plethora of brands made by small independents and giant distilleries, which by far exceed the number of vodkas and whiskies on sale. It is not just in Britain where gin dominates the spirits sector; this is a global phenomenon with unprecedented sales growth.

What is gin? That depends on who you ask. Is it one of the most beloved alcoholic drinks in the world? Is it the enticing potation that makes the senses soar by its combination of exotic botanicals? Is it the signal that the party is starting? Is it the spirit that through a mere sniff evokes a flashback to an excruciating hangover? Is it the base of the most perfect cocktails ever conceived? In reality, it is all of them.

But what is it, really? Gin is flavoured alcohol that starts with the fermentation of sugars sourced from plant materials such as cereals and fruits. During this process, yeast converts sugar to alcohol. The fermented liquid is then distilled and this concentrates its strength. This neutral base spirit has almost no flavour, but the introduction of juniper berries (actually the seed cones of a coniferous tree) imbues it with magic. Gin distillers are magicians and, in addition to juniper, their handbook of potions includes a cornucopia of fruits, roots, flowers, herbs and spices. Most distillers will include between six and twenty different ingredients in their recipe, some of which have a distinct impact on taste. Others are there for practical purposes, or because they sound enigmatic and help to give the gin a point of difference when marketing the brand.

So what do the most popularly used botanicals endow? And are they noticeable? (Yes, they are!)

☞ Juniper is pine-flavoured and also adds spice and fruitiness. It is the primary flavouring ingredient of gin.

☞ Coriander seeds impart spice, lemon and a herbal note. They also act as a flavour fixative (binding volatile aromas and flavours together to prevent them from evaporating).

☞ Citrus fruit peel confers freshness and zest.

☞ Angelica root gives an earthy, woody, dry character and is also a flavour fixative.

☞ Cassia bark contributes a spicy and woody flavour.

☞ Orris root is bitter, earthy and floral. It is the root of the Florentine Iris but it is rarely used for flavouring. Instead it appears in gin because of its ability to bind the other flavours together.

☞ Cardamom imparts spice and citrus.

☞ Cubeb berry is a member of the pepper family and adds a spicy character.

☞ Grains of Paradise are part of the ginger family and have a peppery heat.

☞ Nutmeg bestows a sweet spicy woodiness and is also a flavour fixative.

No other spirit has the astonishing narrative and cultural impact of gin. No other spirit has ridden such a reputational rollercoaster, from Mother's Ruin and the Gin Craze of its early years to the urbane and indispensable star of the drinks cabinet it is today. No other spirit comes close to the excitement and buzz that gin arouses in its acolytes.

Gin evolved in London in the 1690s from a Dutch spirit called genever. That was before Britain became the

United Kingdom of Great Britain through the Act of Union 1707. For the sake of brevity, rather than refer to England, Scotland and Wales, I use the collective term Britain even if it denotes a time before 1707.

The foundations of gin's surprising saga are the myriad reasons to drink it, including religion, politics, patriotism, trade, warfare, economics, desperation, addiction, medicine, empire building, Prohibition and fashion.

So mix yourself a G & T and prepare to meet Madam Geneva and celebrate her awesome power.

HAPPILY EVER AFTER

Why we drank gin: Conviviality, Fellowship, Pleasure

IF YOU WALK up to the bar in London's Viaduct Tavern, do not be surprised to see a member of staff brandishing an ice pick and chipping away at a large block of ice, then placing the chunks into tall stemmed glasses that resemble goldfish bowls. She is in the first stage of mixing Gin & Tonics for a group of men and women. These are not the G & Ts of yesteryear though; they are inspired by the Spanish technique of creating this international cocktail, in an oversized, ice-filled balloon glass known as *copa de balon*, resplendent with garnishes. The customers look on as she assembles the various elements of their potations. It takes time, but the action is entertaining and the anticipation is part of the enjoyment.

The Viaduct Tavern (pictured overleaf) is no ordinary pub. It dates from the mid-nineteenth century and is a modern-day gin palace, offering an array of (mostly) boutique brands, as well as an ever-changing selection

of imaginative gin infusions. Concoctions flavoured by quince, smoked ginger and Szechuan pepper are guaranteed to evince an 'ooh'. One corner of the bar resembles an apothecary's, with lines of jars containing mysterious-looking discs which turn out to be slices of dehydrated lime and grapefruit, and a wooden cupboard, drawers jam-packed with cocoa nibs, lavender and liquorice.

When all the G & Ts are ready, the group sits down at a table, glasses are clinked and everyone takes a sip. There is silence for a few seconds, then comes a cacophony of 'wow', 'delicious' and 'blooming gorgeous'. They all swap glasses and each person samples the others' choices. Conversation and enthusiasm ensue about their cocktails.

That would not happen if they were drinking vodka, and yet technically gin is flavoured vodka, a neutral base spirit seasoned by juniper and – depending on the distiller's recipe – fruits, spices, roots, herbs and flowers. What is it about gin that provokes the excitement described above? It's not just the flavour that prompts this gusto. It is a combination of factors: the exoticism and variety of gin's components, the bonding nature of booze, the shared experience, the sociability and not least the ritual of communal enjoyment of alcohol.

Gin, and the reverence it elicits, epitomise the *Oxford English Dictionary* definition of the word libation:

'the pouring out of a drink as an offering to a deity'

Ancient humans drank alcohol in their worship of the divine. Some religions still do; think of Judaism and Christianity with sacramental wine. The vestiges of pagan rituals and alcohol manifest themselves even today in the ceremony that results when sharing a bevvy. And gin, because it is so much more than mere ethanol, is high on the scale of ritualistic beverages. It lends itself perfectly as a tipple for mixing; mixing means cocktails, and cocktails exist for imbibing in company.

Drinking alcohol is an activity that has no boundaries of class or culture; it is a *lingua franca* that connects humans, regardless of language. Throughout history it has been a social lubricant, used to build relationships, for sealing contracts, as medicine, as an escape, a painkiller, a sterilant, and for celebrations and socialising.

I asked friends to explain what gin means to them. Their answers affirmed the ceremonial nature of gin and its transportive ability. These responses would ring bells in a gin focus group and send the brand owners scrambling to incorporate the findings in marketing campaigns.

☞ 'Every time I have a gin it becomes an occasion. You never just slosh it into a glass like wine. There is a certain amount of pageantry in creating it.'

☞ 'When I have a gin I feel as if I am in an Agatha Christie novel. It is seductive, hedonistic, slightly dangerous and very sophisticated.'

☞ 'When I taste gin from different parts of the
world, it is like a little flavour microcosm of that
area. Some gins can almost transport you to
another place.'

Gin has gone through an extraordinary renaissance. From
the 1960s until the turn of the millennium vodka was the
modish spirit and gin was old hat, something that your
granny sipped. The fact that Britain's Queen Mother was
well known to be partial to a drop did not help to endear
it to a younger, fashionable demographic. Despite its regal
connections, by the early 1980s only a handful of gin distilleries still operated in the UK, producing brands that had
been around for centuries and further reinforcing the per-
ception that gin was passé.

Then Bombay Sapphire was unveiled, and everything
changed. The imagery of Queen Victoria and a perceived
Indian connection gave the impression of longevity, so it
was hard to believe this was a contemporary brand. Its
eye-catching, blue glass bottle, redolent of the Star of India
sapphire, one of the largest such gems ever discovered, was
not just thrown together; it was designed to communicate
style and looked fabulous on the bar shelves of hip cocktail lounges. Crucially the recipe was delicate and floral,
and juniper was not dominant, so for people used to the
neutral taste of vodka, it did not overwhelm the palate. It
did not matter that words such as 'Grains of Paradise' were

unfamiliar to most buyers, because they sounded exotic. Suddenly gin was sexy.

Heritage distillers were prompted to craft original premium gins. This, in turn, inspired the development of independent distilleries making gin on a small scale, but with a big impact on the public consciousness.

Love and marriage, horse and carriage, Gin & Tonic. Before the gin revival happened, little or no thought was given to tonic water. Yet the bulk of a G & T is the 'T', and, if it is composed of artificial flavours, the cocktail will be spoiled, even if the gin is top quality. Today, a new wave of producers are taking tonic seriously, using real ingredients such as elderflower, rose petals, rhubarb and lemongrass.

These are happy and glorious times to be a gin lover, but it was not always so. There were periods when gin was maligned as a destructive force, a devilish havoc-causing concoction. The shift from such censure to the acclaim that gin now enjoys illustrates a triumph of reputation reversal. That journey is a remarkable tale.

GIN TONICA

Topa! to the chefs in northern Spain for gifting the world the Gin Tonica. In 2008 a trend for G & T served in an ice-filled glass and garnished with a variety of fruits, flowers, herbs and spices emerged in the Basque region. This creative serve, and the visual splendour of the *copa de balon*, has adorned Instagram feeds around the globe. There are practical reasons for each element of a Gin Tonica. Large chunks of ice packed together do not melt quickly and dilute the cocktail, while a long-stemmed glass avoids heat from the hand warming the liquid, the shape traps aromas and the choice of garnish enhances the gin.

MEET MADAM GENEVA

Why we drank gin: Patriotism, Escape

Gin, that most British of spirits, is globalisation in a glass, because the botanicals that flavour it are sourced from lands including Morocco, Italy, Germany, China, Indonesia and West Africa. But the only truly British thing about it is the willingness of Britons to take something from overseas and change it slightly to suit their habits.

It developed out of genever (also spelled jenever), a beverage which was widely produced in the Low Countries – the area now known as Belgium, Luxembourg and the Netherlands – from the late sixteenth century. It was distilled from malted cereal and flavoured by juniper berries, and sometimes aniseed and caraway. The name stems from *jeneverbes*, the Dutch word for juniper (in Latin *Juniperus communis*), a coniferous tree that grows extensively in the northern hemisphere. No one can pinpoint the moment of genever's invention; rather, it developed over decades in a number of countries.

English Gin.

If trouble should chance to assail you,

& Fortune in malice should grin,

The cordial that, never will fail you,

Is Seagers & Evans's Gin.

For centuries Europe was in a constant state of turmoil as the dominant nations engaged in struggles over power and religion. For 158 years during the sixteenth to eighteenth centuries the Low Countries were controlled by Spain. Spanish rule was repressive, and it was also Catholic. In the northern part of the region, largely populated by Protestants, the occupation was especially unpopular. Bloody uprisings led by Prince William I, founder of the House of Nassau-Orange, eventually expelled the reviled occupying forces during the Dutch War of Independence. The United Provinces of the Netherlands was formed in 1581 with a proud sense of Protestant identity.

In 1602 the Dutch East India Company was established to trade in Southeast Asia. Colonisation of territories such as the Indonesian archipelago gave the United Provinces a monopoly on commodities that were unobtainable elsewhere. Trade transformed the fortunes of the country, facilitated by its mighty navy and geographical location, with transport links by land to continental Europe and by sea to the rest of the world.

Dutch genever distillers welcomed the novel comestibles from overseas, which were so effective at masking the unpalatable qualities of the rough spirit that production methods of that era dictated. It could not be described as anything other than firewater, but even so, genever was a source of national pride especially as the exceptional botanicals available from Dutch territories in Southeast Asia made it unlike the drinks of any other country.

In Britain there had been an eager consumption of 'strong waters', as distillates were known, for decades, and enthusiasm grew in the party atmosphere that followed the restoration of the monarchy in 1660. It was not unknown for devious distillers to manufacture spirit from worthless beer dregs, hogwash (waste food) and spoiled wine in order to augment pricier materials. Tipplers with financial means consumed imported brands including Dutch genever. It was better quality and it found willing advocates.

In 1688 the most significant factor in the adoption of gin in Britain occurred: the Glorious Revolution, or, depending on your politics and religion, a foreign invasion by an enemy force. At the behest of British parliamentarians and aristocrats, the Protestant Prince William of Orange (grandson of the William who founded the United Provinces of the Netherlands) landed in England, escorted by thousands of soldiers in a fleet of hundreds of ships with the intention of replacing the Catholic King James II. William had a claim on the throne through his marriage to Mary, daughter of James, and they reigned together until her death in 1694, after which he ruled alone. Genever, the beloved libation of the Netherlands, suddenly had a high profile in Britain. The numerous Dutch citizens who had accompanied William needed no encouragement in demonstrating their patriotism, zealously imbibing it and ensuring genever was the most fashionable drink of the day.

One of the first laws passed by William in 1690 was 'An act for the distilling of brandy and spirits from corn'. Corn was a generic term for cereal and did not refer specifically to maize. The law increased duties on beer and imported spirits, reduced the tax on those distilled from British grain and permitted anyone who purchased an inexpensive permit to distil genever. William's act had the effect of ingratiating himself with Britain's landed gentry and securing a market for their crops. Most importantly, it raised funds for the Treasury. For everyone who had a vested interest, his action was a winner – with happy landowners and bulging coffers at the Exchequer – but it had the unintended consequence of more than doubling sales of geneva (juniper spirit distilled in Britain) within sixteen years, and precipitating a devastating social problem called the Gin Craze or Gin Frenzy, which lasted for around 150 years in Britain's major port cities such as Bristol, Portsmouth and, especially, London. The best-known contemporaneous social commentary is the engraving 'Gin Lane' by William Hogarth (pictured overleaf), published in 1751 and inspired by the London parish of St Giles-in-the-Fields, which was the epicentre of destitution. It depicts a nightmare vision of gin's detrimental effect. The central figure is portrayed as a woman slumped on stone steps, who is too drunk to notice

GIN LANE.

that the baby she was holding has tumbled from her arms.
Skeletal figures clutching flagons of gin haunt the picture,
portraying a disturbing way of life that few willingly chose.

Seventeenth-century Britain was a boon for anyone
keen to try novel tastes. Coffee, chocolate and tea made

their debuts, but they were luxuries and therefore prohibitively expensive. In contrast geneva cost mere pennies. By the early eighteenth century the word 'gin' was in use, and the spirit was notorious for its association with London's heavy-drinking underclass, which included women, too, contradicting the popular notion that females did not care for tippling.

A recurring motif in the story of gin is deprivation, and the assumption that only the poor drank it. While they did comprise the majority of quaffers – and the subject of most of the sensationalised headlines – gin was consumed by all classes, albeit discreetly by those of higher status. Like all spirits, genever had started out as a stalwart of domestic medicine cabinets. Juniper-based spiritous potions continued to be supplied by respectable apothecaries, regardless of the mayhem that gin was causing in some sections of society.

Britain was becoming urbanised, as countless people left rural villages and headed to cities to pursue work, prospective partners and new experiences. London, Europe's largest city of half a million inhabitants, was dynamic, bustling, exciting, crowded, filthy, crime-ridden, challenging and polarised by vast wealth alongside dire poverty. The availability of suitable jobs, living wages and decent housing did not keep pace with the increase in population. Slums, nicknamed rookeries, were unspeakably grim, crammed with dilapidated buildings from the medieval era, in which whole families were packed into single rooms. The structures rarely had natural light because immoral land-lords blocked the windows to avoid paying window tax, and because few of the residents could afford candles the interiors were permanently dark. Rookeries were overcrowded and unhygienic: breeding grounds for disease. There was no sanitation, raw sewage ran in the streets and into water sources, and rotting garbage was paradise for vermin. It was the multitudes on the margins living in those dreadful conditions for whom Madam Geneva, as gin was sardonically titled, became such a favoured escape.

Anyone who wanted to lose themselves in cheap booze need not go far, because in the 1730s there were approximately 1,500 distilleries in London. Most of them were tiny home affairs that did not actually distil anything; rather, people purchased neutral spirit from a dealer and added the flavourings typical of gin. There was no archetypal gin drinker – adults, teenagers and children were tipplers. Even babies were sometimes given a dose to help them sleep. But it was women who were habitually excoriated in media reports of uninhibited, debauched or criminal behaviour kindled by cravings for gin. There was a recurring female identity connected to gin. Madam Geneva, Queen Gin and Mother Gin were some of its aliases, and in cartoons it was portrayed as a bawdy, boozy old crone.

By 1751 there were 17,000 private gin shops in a city of approximately 600,000, and that did not include the pubs and taverns that also sold it. The term 'gin shop' suggests

OCTOBER. ——— Battle of A·gin·court. (Petty France)

a formal retail outlet: they were not. Quite often a gin shop was a private dwelling in a slum. If trouble kicked off there was no professional police force for protection and, even if there had been, most gin shops were illegal, so the operator would have been arrested.

London was floating on a river of gin, and drunkenness was endemic. Gin changed the quaffing habits of Britons because it was high strength and swiftly and intensely intoxicated in a way that beer and cider did not. It was consumed in a different way, too: quickly, almost desperately, and often without pleasure. In terms of the intoxication-to-spend ratio, gin was the best value for money. It came in a choice of sizes: drams, quarts, halves and pints. As a comparison, today's legal measure for spirits in Britain's licensed premises is 25 millilitres. Converted to metric measurements, a pint is 568 millilitres. Downing pints of gin was guaranteed to end badly.

Gin was an egalitarian spirit for anyone who could afford it, and was available twenty-four hours a day, in myriad locations, such as blacksmiths', barbers', chandler's shops, in prisons and, most conveniently, in the street. Hawkers (usually female) were mobile, fleet of foot and saw an opportunity wherever a crowd gathered, including to watch public executions, where gin was eagerly knocked back as the condemned hung from the gallows.

Banish any thought of Londoners standing and chatting leisurely as they enjoyed an *al fresco* gin. Tonic water did not exist and gin was so coarse it had to be gulped down in one shot. The technology required to produce gin that was smooth enough to sip was decades away.

WHAT THE DOCTOR ORDERED

Why we drank gin: Health, Longevity

HUMANS HAVE BEEN distilling for thousands of years but no one knows for sure where or when they began. As early as the eighth century BC Chinese distillers worked with plants to make perfume, anaesthetics and antiseptics. Trade routes to and from China disseminated this skill to the Indian subcontinent and the Middle East, and Alexander the Great's conquests through those lands introduced the know-how of distillation to the Mediterranean region. The Phoenicians traded and colonised widely, and diffused knowledge; ancient Greeks, including the philosopher Aristotle and the poet Nicander, wrote about distillation. Roman naturalist Pliny rhapsodised in his magnum opus *Natural History* about the act of distilling, and wrote: 'Oh wondrous craft of the vices! By some mode or other it was discovered that water itself might be made to intoxicate.'

Arab chemists in Baghdad experimented extensively in the seventh and eighth centuries AD, contributing to the

existing understanding of distilling. A scientist called Jabir Ibn Hayyan, better known as Geber, is credited with the invention of the swan-neck alembic still, the principles of which are used to this day. This type of still consists of three parts: a pot where liquid is heated, and a swan-neck-shaped pipe through which vapours pass into a serpentine coil and then condense in a collecting vessel. Decades later the Persian chemist Al Razi outlined the procedure of distilling wine in his book *Al Asrar* and referred to the liquid as *al-koh'l* which passed into English as alcohol.

To academics the transformation of grapes into distillate was supernatural and the word 'spirit' signifies that magic. They shared their expertise among European universities, monasteries and apothecaries. It was especially useful for the last because distilled alcohol is an effective agent for preserving medicinal botanicals. Compounds dissolved in alcohol enter the bloodstream quickly. Alcohol also releases opioid endorphins in the brain and confers a feeling of elation. Although at this time spirits were not consumed for leisure, the side effects of intoxication would have been a pleasing bonus.

The first written proof of the concoction that evolved into gin came from mid-eleventh-century monks at a monastery in Salerno, Italy, who wrote about their research on juniper berries in distilled wine. Juniper has been used for millennia to treat ailments including digestive problems, kidney and gastrointestinal infections, menstrual pain, gout and tapeworms. It was used to purify blood and as an antiseptic, and juniper branches were burned as a fumigant. Herbalist Nicholas Culpeper wrote of juniper in his book *The English Physitian* published 1652 advising of its efficacy in curing a number of ailments including sciatica, convulsions and tuberculosis. Culpeper earned the moniker 'The People's Herbalist' because his inexpensive publications gave crucial information about commonly sourced healing plants to those on limited income unable to afford a doctor. By the time genever became popular in Britain, juniper was already widely used in healthcare.

Juniper also had sacred associations. Middle Eastern Semitic tribes of the tenth century BC associated the tree

with Asherah, their primary goddess. Juniper and fertility were connected. The berries were prescribed for safe and quick delivery during childbirth. This is noteworthy because historically juniper had a reputation as an abortifacient and is the reason for one of gin's aliases: Mother's Ruin. Before abortion was legalised in Britain (1967) it was common to attempt to end an unwanted pregnancy by swigging a bottle of gin and sitting in an extra-hot bath. Some health specialists advise against the consumption of juniper by women who want to be, or who are, pregnant, because it can induce uterine contractions leading to miscarriage.

As distillation spread through Europe via medical schools and universities, alchemists were improving the technique. Florentine medical professor Taddeo di Alderotti is credited with developing fractional distillation, in which a liquid is separated into its component parts. In the late thirteenth century he wrote a treatise called *De Virtute Aquae Vitae quae etiam dicitur aqua ardens* ('On the virtues of the water of life which is also called burning water'), bestowing the name by which distillate is still known. *Aqua vitae* translates into French as *eau de vie*, and into Gaelic as *uisge beatha* (pronounced 'ishky bah': the origin of the word whisky), all of which mean 'water of life'. Professor di Alderotti was convinced that he had discovered the elixir of life, a miraculous treatment for ensuring good health and longevity, when he described distillate

Liber de arte Distil

landi de Compositis.

Das büch der waren kunst zu distillieren die

Composita vñ simplicia/ vnd dz Büch thesaurus pauperũ/ Ein schatz d armẽ ge=
nãt Micariũ/ die brösamlin gefallen võ dẽ büchern d Artzny/ vnd durch Experimẽt
võ mir Jheronimo brũschwick vff geclubt vñ geoffenbart zu trost denẽ die es begerẽ.

thus: 'Its glory is inestimable, it is the parent and lord of all medicines and its effects are marvellous'.

Medics really did believe that *aqua vitae* was a wonder drug and fervently recommended it for a panoply of conditions. In his book *Liber de arte distillandi: De Simplicibus* ('the little book of distillation') Strasbourg-born medic and alchemist Hieronymus Brunschwig (*c*.1450–*c*.1512) wrote about it as being 'the mistress of medicines'. He enlightened readers on some of its benefits. 'It comforts the heart … It eases the pain in the teeth and causes sweet breath … It heals baldness and causes the hair well to grow, and kills lice and fleas. It cures lethargy … It causes good digestions and appetite for to eat, and takes away belching … It purifies the five wits of melancholy and of all uncleanness.'

As news of this fabled panacea spread, apothecaries began to lose their monopoly, because distillation developed into something one could do at home for a regular supply of health-giving tinctures. Affluent households routinely owned a stillatory (a simple still) with which the woman of the house could experiment and create useful concoctions. There was even a helpful manual, *Delightes for Ladies*, published in Britain in 1602 by Sir Hugh Platt, outlining recipes for spirit-based medicinal cordials including juniper as an ingredient.

Naturally the magical combination of something that is good for you *and* that makes you cheerful (i.e. intoxicated) transformed spirits from merely medicinal to recreational.

Demand increased in countries across Europe, prompting the necessity for commercial production and distribution. This was a windfall for Dutch distillers, who were leading exponents of the craft and who already produced genever on a large scale. Existing trading links between the United Provinces and many European countries including Britain meant that genever could easily be procured and was a favoured alternative to French brandy. In Albion, whose eternal enemy was France, it was not just the raw spirit that boosted the popularity of genever; it was raw politics, too, because war was coming.

HOW DOES DISTILLATION WORK?

Distillation concentrates alcohol derived from fermented fruits, cereals and other natural sources of sugar. The conversion of the fermented liquid (wash) into spirit happens in a still, and there are several types, with the continuous still and the pot still being the most commonly used for gin. A continuous still is constructed of connected columns called the analyser and the rectifiers. Steam is pumped into the bottom of the analyser and rises to meet cold wash entering from the top of the column. The steam heats the wash, and the alcohol it contains is vaporised and rises up the analyser, then drops into a rectifier column. Vapours condense on metal plates. The resulting liquid, the descendant of the *aqua vitae* that medieval chemists defined as the elixir of life, has almost no taste. Before it can be classified as gin, it must be flavoured by juniper and other ingredients such as citrus peel, coriander and peppercorns.

To do this, the base spirit is redistilled in a pot still. As the spirit boils, vapours rise through a hanging basket of botanicals, and their aromas and flavours attach to the vapour, which cools in the condenser and turns into liquid. This high-strength spirit is now gin and is ready to be diluted by water to lower its Alcohol by Volume (ABV).

THE BLACK DEATH

During the Black Death of the fourteenth century doctors resembled monstrous creatures because, while treating patients, they wore leather masks with protruding beaks, into which were packed juniper and medicinal herbs that were believed to prevent the plague. In the medieval era most illnesses were blamed on bad air, so fragrant plants and flowers were thought to protect against disease. No one knew at the time that fleas spread the plague but that they were repelled by juniper.

WAR IS THE TRADE
OF KINGS

Why we drank gin: Warfare, Politics, Religion

For Britain, the centuries between the end of Roman rule (AD 410) and the Second World War (1939–45) were characterised by almost continuous warfare, either on home soil or overseas. War was prosecuted for ego, religious beliefs, power, revenge, wealth, politics and territory. When diplomacy failed, monarchs resorted to conflict.

A central character in the history of gin was Prince William of Orange (pictured opposite), later to be King William III. He was involved in numerous conflicts including four against France, ruled at that time by his nemesis King Louis XIV. During hostilities Britain was in turn an enemy and ally of the Dutch; for two of these wars William, as King, was the Commander-in-Chief. A common denominator of these confrontations was religious conflict: Protestant versus Catholic. William was recognised as a champion of Protestantism, determined to give papist Louis a bloody nose. He punished France; not only on the battlefield, but

WILHEM HENRICK PRINS VAN ORANJE EN VAN NASSOV etc.
STADT-HOVDER CAPITEYN ADMIRAEL GENERAEL DER VEREENIGHDE NEDERLANDEN.

economically, too. In Britain, French products including wine and brandy had punitive taxes levied on them, the objective being to price them out of the market. At the same time William's law to encourage distillation of spirits from British-grown cereal, and the associated income from excise duties and sale of alcohol licenses, resulted in a lucrative source of revenue to fund his incessant battles. For a Protestant, the act of drinking genever was a religious and patriotic duty. Brandy belonged to Catholic grape-growing countries, whereas genever was created using cereal, and the European grain-growing countries were largely Protestant. Choice of spirit was holy war by proxy.

Soldiers fighting alongside or against Dutch forces in the mid-to-late seventeenth century were well acquainted with genever. For most of them, this was their first experience of strong waters, with beer or cider being the normal grog. Dutch soldiers were known to fuel up on genever before fighting the enemy. It gave them confidence, rendered them fearless and was also an effective painkiller. British military personnel copied this habit of boozing before battle, a custom later termed 'Dutch courage'.

Britain had no standing army, so where did the warriors required for this incessant combat come from? Officers bought their commission for the prestige and opportunities it afforded, but the troops were recruited: men who for economic reasons joined up to escape penury. They were fed regularly and watered with small beer and diluted rum or gin. Small beer was a low-alcohol brew that refreshed rather than intoxicated. As long as drunkenness was controlled, the top brass considered soldiers quaffing together to be a morale booster that engendered a sense of camaraderie. What about the Navy? In the Age of Sail (mid-sixteenth to mid-nineteenth century), when so much trade, exploration and warfare depended on ships, recruiting and retaining the vital crew frequently made impressment necessary. This was the system of taking men against their will to serve on ships. It was carried out by the Impress Service, more familiarly titled 'press gangs'. By law, they could take only men who had seafaring experience, including merchant seamen and fishermen, although in times of emergency they occasionally took landlubbers. The most useful locations for their prey were dockside pubs and gin shops, where mariners gathered to sup. A drunken sailor was easy pickings.

By 1750 Londoners were guzzling an astounding 11 gallons (50 litres) of gin per capita annually. That number was an average, so disregards the majority of the middle and upper classes who, because gin was *declassé* and associated with anti-social behaviour and criminality, partook on the quiet and in lower volumes. This means that many people were consuming more than 11 gallons a year. The alarming truth was that most gin was consumed by the poverty-stricken, who subsidised the government through the taxes on their tipples. Wars were hugely expensive, and by the end of the eighteenth century the country had been involved in five high-level conflicts, including the American War of Independence.

Britain's rulers faced a conundrum. They could not ignore the damage that addiction to gin was wreaking, but neither could they ignore the money collected as gin duty. To complicate the issue, many Members of Parliament were also influential cereal-growing landowners, who earned significant profits selling their grain to distillers. They had a stake in maintaining an excessive intake of gin and were a formidable lobby.

Officials eventually acknowledged that gin was a scourge on society and responded by passing eight Acts

TOP OF THE GIN LEAGUE

For twenty months from 1762 British forces occupied Manila and the port of Cavite in the Philippines, which were at the time colonial possessions of Spain. Strategically, they benefited Britain's regional interests. Goods including casks of gin travelled in and out of the port, and, when the British withdrew, they left behind a taste for gin amongst the locals. From little acorns grow mighty oaks, because in the twenty-first century the world's biggest consumers of gin are Filipinos, accounting for over 40 per cent of total worldwide gin consumption.

Filipinos have a ritualistic drinking culture called Tagayan, during which friends and family gather for a jollification. A glass is filled with gin (or another spirit) by a *tanggero* – the nominated pourer – and then ritualistically emptied onto the ground as an offering to the ancestors. The glass is refilled, and the *tanggero* passes it to the person next to them to be downed. This is repeated until everyone in the group has imbibed. Sharing the vessel signifies fellowship and trust.

of Parliament between 1729 and 1751, the purpose being to control gin through increasing duty and by raising the price of the license required to sell it. There was another factor too: alcoholics were generally unhealthy. Women gave birth to puny babies who, if they survived, grew up to be puny adults. Infant mortality was so high that one in five children died before their second birthday. The authorities were forced to act by moral outrage, by economics and by the exigencies of war. Britain needed robust men on the battle-field and hardy labourers to work to support the domestic economy and not the feeble and unproductive specimens in thrall to Madam Geneva.

WHEN BUYING A ROUND
WAS BANNED

The Great War (1914–18) was an opportunity for temperance campaigners
to further their quest. As Chancellor of the
Exchequer and later Prime Minister, the tee-
totaller David Lloyd George succeeded in his
intentions to reduce the rates of tippling by
increasing spirits duty. His most radical policy
was to restrict pub opening hours in cities and
industrial areas. Instead of pubs being allowed
to trade between 5 a.m. and 12.30 a.m. at night,
the new times were 12 p.m. to 2.30 p.m. and
6.30 p.m. to 9.30 p.m. More draconian still
was the ban on buying rounds. It became an
offence punishable by a fine or six months'
imprisonment for anyone caught purchasing
a drink for a person other than themselves. His
strategy was successful, because sales of gin
and other alcohol decreased.

WHAT'S YOUR POISON?

Why we drank gin: Desperation, Addiction

FANCY A GLASS of Scorch Gut, Strip Me Naked or Kill Me Quick? These were some of the early nicknames for gin. Today's gin typically contains alcohol, water, juniper, coriander seeds, citrus and other botanicals. In the eighteenth century it was normal for British gin to contain alcohol in addition to: sulphuric acid; turpentine; laurel water, derived from the leaves of laurel bushes; oil of almond, to mimic the flavour of juniper; and lead acetate for sweetening. Gin bore little resemblance to the Dutch genever from which it had evolved.

The aim of unscrupulous distillers was to substitute costly ingredients and produce gin as inexpensively as possible. Oil of almond, lead acetate and laurel water all contain cyanide, and turpentine and sulphuric acid were present, albeit in low concentrations. The cumulative effect of toxic compounds and substantial amounts of booze consumed regularly, twinned with poor nutrition, insanitary housing

and lack of healthcare, reduced life expectancy. Newspapers habitually reported deaths caused by bingeing pint after pint of gin. During the peak of the Gin Craze the mortality rate was higher than the birth rate, and the population declined because women were often unable to conceive or carry a baby to term, while many men were infertile. From a humanitarian point of view, the negative effects of gin and its associated lifestyle were ruinous, and successive British governments tried to control the epidemic. They were also concerned about the economic and societal cost wrought by gin. On one hand, the Treasury benefited from taxes collected from its production and sale, but, on the other, it was responsible for generations of stunted individuals not fit to work, who lived miserable and blighted lives, and for babies born suffering from foetal alcohol syndrome. Their alcoholic parents were invariably unable to nurture them, so they were abandoned and left for the parish to safeguard. Gin was not the only blame factor, though; the privations of poverty were culpable too.

Especially problematic was unfettered street selling, and, through the passing of the Gin Act 1733, professional informants were hired to hunt down and report unlicensed sales of gin. This was lucrative employment which offered a hefty reward of £5 (worth several hundred pounds today) for each conviction. Rather than reducing criminality, however, it actually increased it, as infuriated gin drinkers took murderous revenge on the state-sponsored spies, with many instances of snitches being beaten to death. On paper, the policy seemed like a good idea, but persuading constables to make arrests was not universally successful. This was prior to the existence of an organised police force, and, at the time, law enforcement was carried out by men who were obliged to volunteer for the role. If it meant detaining their neighbours then they often chose not to do so in order to protect themselves against retribution from violent mobs who made it impossible for the constable to carry out his duty.

The Gin Act of 1736 quadrupled the duty on gin and vastly increased – to £50 – the cost of a license to sell it. That was more than most retailers earned in a year from gin sales, and few could afford the legal document, so they ignored the edict and continued to supply gin under pseudonyms such as 'Cuckold's Comfort'. Some London

publicans were accused of inciting civil disorder when, in response to the new law, rioting broke out, requiring the deployment of troops to quell the turmoil. This Gin Act did temporarily reduce demand in pubs but did nothing to deter illegal sales by unlicensed vendors or legal sales by apothecaries who took advantage of a loophole that meant purveyors of medicinal spirits required no permit.

Tipplers responded to this detested law in a characteristic British way – with satire. In several cities 'mourners' dressed in black staged funerals for Madam Geneva. London's memorial was a procession down Piccadilly behind a gin-laden hearse. Cartoon sketches were published, and the best known depicted a funerary monument displaying the inscription: 'To the mortal memory of

Madam Geneva, who died September 29th 1736. Her weeping servants and loving friends consecrate this tomb.'

Despite the good intentions of the Act, it was not long before the resumption of business as usual. The risk of being rumbled by a grass was ever-present, but the lure of easy money from selling gin was too seductive, and it led to imaginative ways to supply the market surreptitiously. The most ingenious scheme was the Puss & Mew method devised by one Captain Dudley Bradstreet, a chancer always on the look-out for a money-making opportunity. At a dwelling near the Barbican in the City of London he set out his stall in the guise of a cat-shaped wooden board nailed to the window. Punters knocked on the door and whispered 'Puss give me a pennyworth of gin' to which a voice from within replied 'Mew'. The customer then dropped coins into a drawer and positioned a vessel under the cat's paw into which gin trickled from a concealed lead pipe. It was such a money-spinner that Bradstreet claimed to be raking in £20 a week profit. To put that in context, the annual wage of a house maid at the time was around £8. The success of this nascent vending machine spawned copycats around London's gin-swigging districts, and so illicit sales of Madam Geneva continued unabated.

Newspapers of the time printed dramatic reports about depraved behaviour. There were countless instances of murder and manslaughter; men, catatonic through bingeing on gin, who were robbed, and women who were so inebriated and desperate for money to buy more gin that they stripped the clothes off infants to exchange at the pawn shop, leaving the children naked in the street. Unsurprisingly, the opinion of the many was that gin was a corrupter of morals and that the under-privileged could not control their urges.

Despite the passing of more legislation, what finally did reduce sales of Mother Gin was Mother Nature. A series of poor harvests and crop failures in the 1750s led to distillers being banned from using domestically grown cereals, because they were needed instead for baking bread. Wages were depressed, food prices were inflated and the poor had no disposable cash to spend on booze. The worst of the Gin Craze was over, but the public did not cease tippling completely. Social deprivation that led the underclass to seek refuge in a glass did not disappear, and, although they drank less than the zenith of 11 gallons annually, the associated criminality and drunkenness did not decline. Gin was still a menace to the populace least able to afford its deleterious effects.

As London and other industrialised cities grew relentlessly, they enticed streams of town and country folk with the promise of work and opportunities. Just as rural dreamers of the eighteenth century had relocated for the same reasons and taken solace in gin, so their counterparts one hundred years later did the same. Although not as ghastly as the early iterations of gin, the Victorian version still needed additions such as sugar or peppermint to mask the taste,

The Gin Palace.

and it had to be downed swiftly. An intensely flavoured sweet gin called Old Tom remained popular until later in the nineteenth century, when a new style, London Dry, changed expectations of what gin was supposed to be.

In 1825 the British parliament passed the Duty on Spirits Act, which reduced tax by 40 per cent. The aim was to eliminate the widespread criminal smuggling of alcohol, but it had the almost immediate effect of more than doubling gin consumption in Britain. Gin shops and pubs proliferated in cities and towns, and fierce competition led to a newfangled phenomenon: the Gin Palace (pictured on page 47). As usual, the target was those on low income.

Gin Palaces suited their sobriquet. They were gaudy, ostentatious licensed premises that were beacons in a dismal urban landscape. Well-lit and warm, they were a refuge for the masses living in abysmal circumstances. Compared to the squalor of slums, they were luxurious. No expense was spared on marble columns, mosaic décor, brightly coloured majolica tiles, carved mahogany bar serveries, glazed plate glass windows, brass fittings, illuminated clocks and gas lighting. Gin Palaces were located in high footfall, central city areas and designed for a quick turnover. They had few or no chairs and tables: just the occasional hard bench to rest on. This was a new format: vertical drinking with large casks behind the bar, from which gin was decanted into jugs to be poured into small glasses that patrons knocked back.

For a satirical vision of what gin shops and Gin Palaces offered their clientele, look at the drawings, both titled 'The Gin-Shop', published by George Cruikshank in 1829 and 1839. In the earlier work (pictured opposite) a drunken man is handed a glass by a skeleton masquerading as a pretty young bar maid. Next to him, a child drains a measure and an inebriated woman force feeds gin to her baby. Rather than being poured from wooden casks, the gin is served from coffins standing against the wall. In the later drawing (pictured overleaf), a group of customers, dwarfed by vast barrels of gin, stand beneath grand classical columns in a Gin Palace. A gaggle of unkempt men have raised

The Gin-shop.

fists, a child stands by the bar purchasing a bottle of gin, a trio of elderly women sup their drams and a crippled man in rags looks expectantly as his drink is handed over. In real life, this was a typical scene, repeated day in, day out.

Gin Palaces were goldmines. They had extended opening hours from dawn until after midnight and had one purpose: to attract punters and make them spend money. It was not unusual for someone to stroll in, order a penny-worth of gin, chug it and stroll out again within a minute.

According to Charles Dickens' description of Gin Palaces in *Sketches by Boz*, gin was marketed with names such as 'The Good for Mixing', 'Choice Compounds', 'The Real Knock-Me-Down', 'The Cream of the Valley' and 'The Regular Flare-Up'. They varied in strength, and each may have tasted slightly different to the others, but the base spirit was the same.

As well as a novelist, Dickens was a people watcher, journalist, social commentator and pubgoer. He saw first-hand the plight of Britain's gin-addled masses and did not resile from challenging the powerful to improve the lives of the poor, when he wrote in London's Evening Chronicle:

Gin-drinking is a great vice in England, but wretchedness and dirt are a greater; and until you improve the homes of the poor, or persuade a half-famished wretch not to seek relief in the temporary oblivion of his own misery, with the pittance which, divided among his family, would furnish a morsel of bread for each, gin-shops will increase in number and splendour.

Once again the authorities were forced into action. Enter the Beerhouse Act 1830. It gave any rate payer permission to brew and sell beer upon purchase of an inexpensive license. The idea was to stimulate competition on pricing thereby encouraging the public to renounce gin and instead quaff benign and health-promoting beer. Unsurprisingly, it resulted in a raft of new breweries and pubs throughout the country and the population drunk on beer in places where gin was not generally available.

In London and cities where gin-drinking was rife, the Beerhouse Act made an impact, because the cost of beer was now significantly lower than that of gin. Breweries took over Gin Palaces and shifted the focus of them from being mere pitstops for gin. They were reborn as pubs that sold beer and food as well.

Slowly, a change was coming in gin's notoriety, from the drink of the impoverished to that of the affluent and respectable. We can thank the Navy and the discovery of the Cinchona tree for this shift.

A LIFE ON THE
OCEAN WAVE

Why we drank gin: Medicine, Survival, Empire-building

Spain and Portugal were world powers from the fifteenth to the nineteenth century, with vast overseas empires. France, the Netherlands and Britain enviously eyed the wealth accrued and were spurred to seek their own dominions abroad. For the Netherlands this was land in the Americas, Africa and Asia. As one of the leading maritime nations between the sixteenth and eighteenth centuries they had global trading links. Access to valuable commodities from their colonies considerably enriched the Dutch kingdom.

Britain was also in an expansive mood and, from the seventeenth century, its navy planted the flag for Britannia in all hemispheres. London was a trading powerhouse, the river Thames being the equivalent of a superhighway for ships. Its docks adopted nomenclature that reflected the city's international connections. Warehouses in the East and West India Docks were laden with imported goods:

tobacco, ivory and hardwoods, as well as flavoursome food-stuffs that made victuals so much more exciting. Those warehouses also contained botanicals that improved gin immeasurably in the nineteenth century when superior distillation processes were developed.

One circumstance that enhanced Britain's fortunes was the East India Company, formed by London merchants in 1600 to exploit trade in the East. This astonishingly powerful organisation, later to be a de facto government in India, acted on behalf of the British state in the subcontinent for almost 150 years from the early eighteenth century.

Overseas adventures and relentless wars entailed ships being away for months at sea. A lack of fresh food meant a monotonous diet of salted meat and ship's biscuits. This restricted menu of minimal nutrition led to health problems, and chief among them was scurvy. Scurvy is caused by a vitamin C deficiency and, left untreated, is a killer. Symptoms include bleeding in joints and muscles, bleeding gums and lost teeth, reopening of previously healed wounds and heart failure. Scurvy was so severe that it caused the death of hundreds of thousands of mariners, many more than were killed in combat by enemy forces over the years. Various remedies were trialled including the ones favoured by the explorer James Cook: sauerkraut and cider, consumed separately, not together! Eventually the British Admiralty decreed that the most efficient antiscorbutic was citrus fruit, so from 1795 British sailors received a compulsory daily

dose of lemon or lime juice, earning them the nickname 'Limeys'. Ships also carried spirits, not just for drinking but as a sterilant and an analgesic. Someone had the idea of adding gin to lime juice, and lo and behold the Gimlet cocktail was inaugurated. The origin of the name may either stem from the word for the small metal tool used to drill a hole in the wooden barrel of lime juice, or from Sir Thomas Gimlette, Surgeon General of the Navy.

Gimlet was not the only ship-born gin cocktail. Pink Gin also owes its birth to the high seas. Just like the Gimlet, which acted as a prophylactic against scurvy, so Pink Gin was medicine intended to prevent seasickness. The 'pink' refers to bitters which infuse a delicate rose hue. Medicinal bitters, containing plants such as gentians dissolved in alcohol, had been used over centuries for a variety of ailments, including stomach and digestive disorders. In 1824 an entrepreneurial physician, Gottlieb Siegart, based in the Venezuelan port of Angostura (now Ciudad Bolívar), began to market his bitters to visiting mariners. They sold prodigiously, but more so after officers in the British Navy added them to gin and instituted a habit that other seafarers adopted. The combination of gin and medicinal bitters was also embraced by colonists whose stomachs tended to be 'delicate'.

As scurvy was a killer on the high seas, so was malaria for anyone visiting or living in mosquito-infested lands. The holy grail in prevention was the discovery that Cinchona bark, from a forest tree of the Andes, contains quinine. It acts by calming malarial fever and by killing the parasite responsible for the disease. By the 1650s, when Spain controlled much of South America, Cinchona was obtained at a high price from Spanish traders. European doctors recognised its value as a treatment and in 1768 Scottish medic James Lind, the same man who had advised the British Navy that citrus prevents scurvy, recommended a daily shot of Cinchona powder for sailors in the tropics. Finding reliable medication was essential to the national interest of any country fighting wars in, or trading with, malaria-endemic territories. This mainly included Britain, France, the Netherlands, Portugal and Spain. The trouble was that Spain had a monopoly on Cinchona and it was almost a century before British explorers in Ecuador were able to source the seeds and plant them in the subcontinent, where they were successfully propagated, eventually multiplying into vast plantations. The vital role that quinine played in the success of the East India Company cannot be overstated.

To administer Cinchona, its bark was dried, ground and dissolved in alcohol. This procedure was inefficient and wasteful, but early in the nineteenth century French pharmacists Joseph-Bienaimé Caventou and Pierre-Joseph Pelletier solved the problem when they isolated the alkaloids in Cinchona. One of them was quinine; by boiling the bark in sulphuric acid, the resulting quinine sulphate was water soluble, but unpalatably bitter. For colonists this was the cue for a spoonful of sugar to help the medicine go down. It was even better when combined with gin and water. This was a cocktail in the making, but something indispensable was missing.

Carbonated water had been created in Leeds in 1767 by the chemist Joseph Priestley, but it was industrialised by Johann-Jacob Schweppe. He did not invent tonic water, but his company popularised an existing carbonated beverage that contained bitter orange and quinine and Schweppe's version was named Indian Quinine Tonic Water. It was a hit with British colonists, who took quinine daily. Someone unknown to history, possibly in India, decided that a nip of gin would perk up the tonic water and, when lemon – to

Cool Interlude

help dissolve the quinine – and a few chunks of ice were added, the Gin & Tonic debuted as the perfect chotapeg for a hot climate: bitter, refreshing and restorative. Alongside the quinine tonic, gin was living up to its roots as a medicinal tincture and provided the ultimate example of being 'just what the doctor ordered'. G & Ts were also delicious and far too agreeable not to sip for recreation.

Returning colonists brought back to the old country their sociable habit of gathering for a cocktail and when, in the early twentieth century, private gentlemen's clubs, high end restaurants and hotel bars started to serve G & Ts, gin's status as an elegant potation was confirmed. A Gin & Tonic was simple to make and easy to drink, and consequently it turned into the world's favourite cocktail.

This could not have happened without a sea change in the stature of gin. Improvements in manufacturing transformed gin from the poison of the Gin Craze era to a spirit embraced by polite society.

RING IN THE CHANGES

Why we drank gin: Refreshment, Entertainment

All hail Aeneas Coffey and Robert Stein. In 1831 Coffey patented an appliance that was an adaptation of Stein's innovative still that had resulted in more efficient production of alcohol. Until that technological advance, distillers had employed the pot still method, but it was a technique which fostered low-grade spirit. Sugar and flavourings were vital to make it halfway drinkable. The Coffey, known today as the continuous still (pictured opposite), generated a cleaner tasting, high-calibre distillate that required no sweeteners.

Distillers responded to this progress by creating a lighter, more delicate gin that was impossible to make in a pot still. Later in the century it was marketed as London Dry, the dry being a nod to the absence of sweetness. Spirits produced in a Coffey provided a blank canvas on which to experiment with botanicals such as cardamom, nutmeg and orange peel, easily acquired thanks to Britain's worldwide trading links.

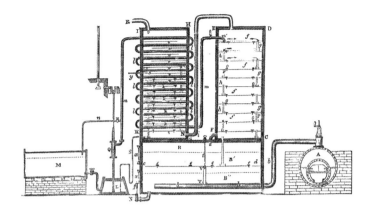

This innovation and improved quality led to the expansion of family distilling businesses. By the 1860s distilleries including Tanqueray (later to form an alliance with Gordon's, which had been founded in the late eighteenth century), Gilbey's, Boodle's and Beefeater, all of which continue to trade today, were, in addition to dozens of now defunct companies, producing London Dry in the UK's capital. These companies manufactured on an industrial scale and had a prominent position in Britain's economy. They formed a cartel to lobby politicians for favourable policies, one of which was immunity from paying export duty. As a result London Dry was exported globally to season the glasses of those unaware of the lurid headlines of gin's previous decades.

An Act of Parliament described as 'An act for granting to Her Majesty certain duties of excise and stamps' was passed in 1861 and was referred to as the Single Bottle Act.

The Sketch

For people who use their brains...

GIN AS GIN SHOULD BE

Gordon's Special Dry London Gin.

Tanqueray Gordon & Limited
The Distillery London

WHITE FOR PURITY
FREE FROM COLOURING MATTER
AND ALL INJURIOUS INGREDIENTS
"LANCET" report on every bottle
THE HEART OF A GOOD COCKTAIL

For over a century and a half GORDON'S GIN has been accepted as the Standard of Quality by which other Gins are judged. It is made as Gin *should* be made — free from colouring matter, free from injurious ingredients. It contains the greatest percentage of those important properties which are considered by the Medical Profession to be most beneficial to the human system.

If you are not already insisting on GORDON'S GIN you should—for your health's sake—do so.

There are no impurities to come through and spoil your Cocktail or Long Drink.

**NO COLOURING MATTER
NO INJURIOUS INGREDIENTS**

Gordon's Gin
—has a larger sale than any other gin in the world

It authorised dealers of spirits to sell their wares in bottles, rather than from the anonymous wooden casks of the past. This also helped to elevate gin's standing, because buyers could trust it had not been contaminated or diluted by the retailer. When exclusive shops such as Fortnum & Mason started to sell bottles of gin, that was the ultimate seal of approval.

It is hard to believe now, given the eminence of Scotch, but until the mid-nineteenth century whisky was considered by the English to be a peasant drink and was not widely consumed south of the Scottish border. Options for spirits were limited to brandy, rum and gin/genever, meaning that, even during the decades of gin's association with the less privileged, it was still consumed by the well-heeled. Punch, for instance, was a cocktail before the term even existed: a combination of whatever spirit was to hand, plus water, sugar, citrus fruit and spices. It was adopted by employees of the East India Company and popularised back in Britain.

The term Punch may derive from a Sanskrit word *pancha*, which means 'five'. It was first recorded in writing in 1632 and characterised as a convivial pick-me-up served from a large porcelain, glass or metal bowl, perfect for communal enjoyment and dispensed by ladling into individual punch cups. By the eighteenth century, when the spirit in the mixture was most likely to have been Old Tom Gin, punch was linked to raucous gatherings of men in clubs,

coffee houses, taverns or dedicated punch-houses, the last
of which were notorious for their louche atmosphere. Once
again, William Hogarth enlightened and entertained society
through his engraving 'A Midnight Modern Conversation'
(pictured above), published in 1733, which shows a group
of dishevelled, drunken men surrounded by empties and
sitting around a table, upon which a capacious punch bowl
is centre stage. Social rank was connected with the design
and size of the bowl, and eighteenth-century punch bowls
were often used to send political messages and allegiances
by way of their decoration. The British Museum owns
one (pictured opposite), dating from 1749, adorned by a
portrait of Bonnie Prince Charlie (Charles Edward Stuart,
the Young Pretender to the throne vacated by James II).
He wears tartan plaid, which is partisan in itself because

Scottish Highland dress had been banned following the Jacobite Uprising of 1745. This involved Prince Charles' supporters, who battled British military forces with the aim of restoring a Stuart to the monarchy that, in their opinion, had been usurped by William of Orange. Jacobites would undoubtedly have proposed toasts to the 'King o'er the water' – the exiled Charles in France – and to 'The little gentleman in the black velvet waistcoat', a reference to the mole that may indirectly have been involved in the death of William following a riding accident when his horse stumbled on a mole-hill.

In the nineteenth century punch was a decorous way to entertain guests, a genteel refreshment for women as well as men. Think scenes in Jane Austen novels, with the protagonist standing by the punch bowl at the ball as the object of her interest stands brooding across the room. Punch was never exclusively for people of wealth, though, as outlined by Charles Dickens when his impoverished characters Mr Micawber and Bob Cratchit took delight in concocting albeit basic versions for celebrations.

In 1840 the sustained popularity of punch inspired James Pimm to introduce his eponymous combination of gin, herbs, spices and fruit as a digestif for diners at his London oyster bar. They needed no persuading that a potion featuring gin was a good idea. A very good idea; try and imagine a British summer without a glass of Pimm's No. 1 Cup and lemonade, garnished by cucumber, citrus fruit, mint and borage.

A disastrous episode in France had the unforeseen consequence of increasing the appeal of gin, when, in 1862, the French wine and brandy industries were decimated by a rapacious aphid *Phylloxera vastatrix*, unwittingly introduced into France when a wine producer planted infected American grapevines in his Rhône valley vineyard. The dry-leaf devastator, as the aphids were nicknamed, feeds on the roots of vines and kills them. *Phylloxera* spread relentlessly throughout the wine regions of Europe, and millions of hectares of vines were destroyed. Not even decades of

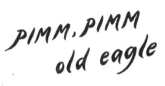

war, when the enemy adopted a scorched-earth policy, were as profoundly damaging to grape-growing countries as this microscopic adversary was. Hundreds of remedies for exterminating the pest were suggested, including holy water, bones dissolved in sulphuric acid, human and horse urine, whale oil and volcanic ash from Pompeii. Only one thing worked: grafting US rootstock that had become immune to *Phylloxera* onto European vines. It took thirty years for large-scale replanting of vineyards and the recovery of the wine industry. During that time, the absence of brandy meant that demand for gin at home and overseas rocketed.

Gin history is British-centric because gin was developed in Britain, but it became internationally beloved, especially in America. Spiritous drinks were a feature of life from the time of the first European settlers. Before Manhattan became New York, it was New Amsterdam, capital city of New Netherland, a colony established in 1624 by the Dutch West India Company. Distillers produced genever in the city, and imports from Old Amsterdam were easily obtainable too. New Netherland was ceded to Britain in 1664 after hostile activity and renamed as the more familiar New York. Juniper-flavoured spirits were customary by the time British distillers began exporting gin to the States, and it was the Americans who helped to establish it as the superstar of the bar. For that, we need to thank the cocktail.

ROLL OUT THE BARREL

Gin's twenty-first-century revival has introduced a plethora of flavours to the palate, including barrel-aged gin or yellow gin – an archaic term that describes the delicate colour that comes from the oak – which have premium credentials for marketeers. After the gin has been distilled, it is decanted into oak barrels to rest for months or years, during which it will be influenced by flavours from the wood. These depend on what liquor the barrel previously contained, for instance bourbon, wine or sherry.

Although it sounds innovative, storing gin in barrels is nothing new because, until glass bottles became the common receptacle for spirits in the nineteenth century, most gin was kept in wooden casks. These were refilled repeatedly, so the oaky, vanilla, nutty character of the wood would have declined over time.

WHERE'S THE PARTY?

Why we drank gin: Cocktail-mania, Rebellion

AMERICANS DID NOT restrict themselves to neat liquor because, by the early nineteenth century, potations going by the generic term cocktails were being enjoyed as a morning energiser, an aperitif, an afternoon treat, an evening relaxant and for other occasions. Just as Madame Lily Bollinger of the renowned Champagne house amusingly described the necessity of sparkling wine – 'I drink champagne when I'm happy and when I'm sad. Sometimes I drink it when I'm alone. When I have company I consider it obligatory. I trifle with it if I'm not hungry and drink it when I am. Otherwise I never touch it unless I'm thirsty' – so cocktails in America were to be consumed for myriad occasions.

Cocktail, as a term connected to alcohol, was first mentioned in a London newspaper in 1798. Its etymology is not clear and there are several theories:

1 It derives from a French word *coquetel*, a mixed wine beverage.

2 It was a mispronunciation of the French word for eggcup, *coquetier*, used for measuring liquid.

3 Cock-tail described a horse with a docked tail that was shaped like a cockerel's fan tail. Tail docking was routinely practised on cross-breed horses.

4 Another equine connection is the discredited habit of 'gingering' a horse: to make it cock its tail and look lively. It involves inserting a piece of ginger or rubbing ginger paste into the horse's anus.

Americans enjoyed a cornucopia of cocktails including Gin Sling, Sherry Cobbler, and Timber Doodle. They were presented in glass, rather than ungainly vessels of earthenware or pewter, and cooled by a liberal addition of ice. American bartenders were renowned for their inventive mixing skills, and top of the league was Jeremiah 'Jerry' Thomas (pictured overleaf), an inveterate showman who travelled the world demonstrating his expertise, publicising his manual *The Bartender's Guide: How to Mix Drinks, or, The Bon Vivant's Companion* and promoting the latest fashion for mixology. Many of his recipes contained gin, and one of them was similar to the cocktail that arguably did more to sex up the reputation of gin than anything else. Enter the Martini, where gin met French vermouth and was garnished with an olive. It was the marriage of juniper, wine, herbs and spices that launched a thousand London Dry-laden ships headed to ports the world over. When the V-shaped stemmed glass

became *de rigueur* in the early twentieth century, the Martini was already a symbol of sophistication. Several stories circulated about the provenance of the Martini, and Jerry Thomas played a central role, but there is no contemporaneous evidence to confirm any of them. The truth is that no-one knows who first stirred a Martini, and where.

As Americans were enjoying their cocktails, the abstinence movement was marshalling support, initially led by the Woman's Christian Temperance Union and later by the Anti-Saloon League. To them, booze contributed to a raft of social problems. Members were so successful at lobbying politicians that an amendment to the US Constitution was ratified in 1919 with the goal of banning intoxicating liquor. This led to the National Prohibition Act, aka the Volstead Act (after the Chair of the House Judiciary Committee). Its purpose was to regulate the manufacture, sale, barter and transportation of intoxicating beverages stronger than 0.5 per cent ABV, but at the same time to ensure adequate supplies of alcohol for industry, medicine, science and religious rituals. Noticeable by its absence in the new law was the sanction against actually partaking of alcohol, because that would have criminalised communion wine.

On 16 January 1920 the Noble Experiment, better known as Prohibition, began, and legal bars, saloons and taverns were forced to cease trading. This naturally led to the establishment of speakeasies, which were illicit joints selling illegal hooch. The name possibly derived from the warning to speak quietly so as not to attract the police, or from the early nineteenth-century British slang phrase 'speak easy shop' to denote a place where smuggled goods were sold. Speakeasies turned into the beating heart of social life for a section of American society. In some states they were called blind tigers or blind pigs, from the practice of charging a fee to see something unusual, perhaps an animal, and then giving customers a complimentary tipple, thereby taking advantage of the loophole in the law that drinking alcohol was not a criminal offence, but buying it was.

It was almost impossible for law enforcement to patrol such a vast country and, as any ruling power throughout antiquity who has attempted to ban intoxicants might grudgingly admit: if humans want to quaff, they will always find a way of doing so. Organised crime recognised that and, consequently, the Mafia and other criminal gangs cashed in and reaped huge profits by distributing boot-legged liquor during the thirteen years of Prohibition. The term 'bootleg' may derive from the custom of hiding valuables or contraband inside high-leg boots. With it came violence, extortion, bribery of public officials and an increase in gambling and prostitution. In other words, social disorder.

Anyone seeking a snifter could easily find it and knew where the party was. Speakeasies were exciting, dangerous and unlike anything else in the USA. Some of them were basic back rooms or cellars, while others were more luxe, and for those the clientele dressed up for a real night out because, as well as cocktails, some venues sold food, and some hosted bands playing music and dancing showgirls. Three of New York's estimated 30,000 speakeasies – El Morocco, the Stork Club and the Cotton Club – went on to become the city's leading nightclubs after Prohibition was repealed. Many urban spots were integrated, mean-ing that people of diverse races and colours mingled, and both sexes socialised on equal terms. For women, this was a liberation. They were actively welcomed in

speakeasies, where they had freedom to behave in a manner that American attitudes of the era denied them. Some started working as bartenders and hostesses, and some even owned speakeasies themselves. This was the Jazz Age, and it presented a vision of an America emancipated from the strictures promoted by evangelical Protestants who espoused the ban on alcohol.

The majority of liquor sold in speakeasies was Bathtub Gin, served in the form of cocktails to cover the wretched taste of industrial spirit. By the terms of the Volstead Act, the creation of that type of spirit was not illegal, because it was required for a variety of purposes including medicine, cleaning, explosives and fuel. Gin lent itself to the bathtub treatment because it is a flavoured spirit, and adding flavour extracts to base spirit gave the impression that it was actually gin. The origin of the moniker 'bathtub' is unclear. It could be because bottles of spirit too tall for a basin were stood up in a bath to be diluted, or it may be that gin was blended with flavourings in a bath and bottled from there. It was best not to think about what was in it, because industrial spirit was denatured according to rules laid down by the US Government. Denaturing involved the addition of chemicals such as kerosene, petrol and acetone to render the spirit undrinkable. Criminal gangs stole millions of gallons of denatured spirit and employed chemists to renature and redistil it, and make it potable. If they were successful then the spirit was not lethal, but if they did not remove all the poisonous additives then drinkers could die, and hundreds did so. This was a scandal because the authorities knew of the deaths, but they continued to rule that legally produced spirit must be tainted by toxins to thwart people from consuming it.

As well as distributing prodigious amounts of hooch, the Mafia smuggled premium liquor including Scotch whisky and British gin through the USA's lengthy coastline and porous borders with Canada and Mexico, so the good stuff could be sourced for a price. A successful ruse was for liquor-laden ships to moor in international waters and act as off-licences to supply smaller boats that sailed from the mainland. Further jinks on the high seas happened on 'the cruises to nowhere', more accurately termed booze cruises, which provided a venue for legal quaffing outside America's territorial waters as ships sailed aimlessly off the American coast.

Judging by the blatant disregard that so many Americans had for Prohibition, a more accurate description for the period should have been 'Permission'. In addition to hundreds of thousands of speakeasies across the country, alcohol could be bought in a multitude of locations such as drugstores, tea-rooms, vegetable markets and laundries. Even President Warren Harding, who as a Senator had voted in favour of Prohibition, was known to sup with colleagues in the Oval Office. If the big chief was tippling then how could law-makers expect other citizens to resist the urge? They could not, so in 1933 the law was revoked. By then Franklin D. Roosevelt was resident in the White House and, each day before dinner, he hosted a cocktail party, mixing the Martinis himself.

Cocktail parties were an enduring legacy of Prohibition. With the demise of Bathtub Gin and the legal availability of superior British gin, the Martini, which essayist and cultural commentator H. L. Menken defined as 'the only American invention as perfect as the sonnet', was once again the symbol of style. The 'gintelligensia' of satirists, poets and writers such as Dorothy Parker and F. Scott Fitzgerald (whose fictional character Jay Gatsby earned his vast fortune through bootlegging) glamorised the Martini to the extent that it became *the* motif for modernity.

QUEEN GIN

Why we drank gin: Glamour, Sophistication, Fashion

As Americans endured the privations of the Volstead Act, Londoners and Parisians benefited from an exodus of US cocktail-making maestros who moved to Britain and France to find work. In London that was in swish hotels such as the Savoy, home of the celebrated American Bar. Located in theatreland, it was the haunt of actors, film stars and singers. Mixologists were centre stage, presenting a theatrical performance as they worked their craft. This was the Roaring Twenties, when fun, frivolity and hedonism were the priority, and affluent party-loving young socialites nicknamed the Bright Young Things chose Gin & It (Italian Vermouth) as their cocktail of choice. Much as in today's celebrity culture, the mainstream media was obsessed by the Bright Young Things and their habits, which influenced the wider public. Gin, cocktails and glamour were inextricably linked.

Nothing could dazzle like the Hollywood film industry and, when much-admired actors were shown sipping gin,

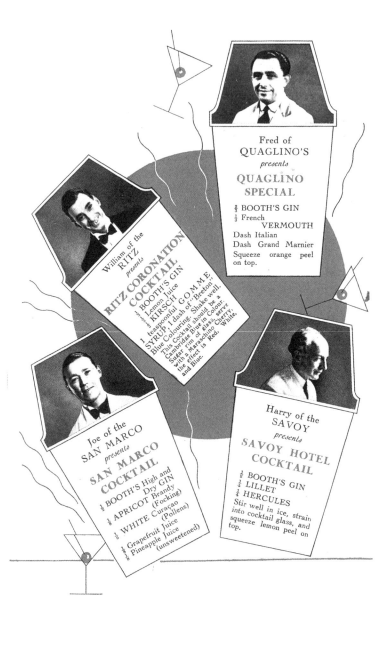

Fred of
QUAGLINO'S
presents

**QUAGLINO
SPECIAL**

⅔ BOOTH'S GIN
⅓ French
VERMOUTH
Dash Italian
Dash Grand Marnier
Squeeze orange peel
on top.

William of the
RITZ
presents

**RITZ CORONATION
COCKTAIL**

⅓ BOOTH'S GIN
⅓ Lemon Juice
⅓ KIRSCH
1 teaspoonful GOMME
SYRUP. 1 dash of
Blue Colouring. Shake well.
This Cocktail should be a
Cambridge Blue in Colour.
Sugar rim of glass; serve
with a Maraschino Cherry,
the effect is Red, White,
and Blue.

Joe of the
SAN MARCO
presents

**SAN MARCO
COCKTAIL**

⅓ BOOTH'S High and
Dry GIN
⅓ APRICOT Brandy
(Focking)
⅓ WHITE Curaçao
(Pollens)
⅓ Grapefruit Juice
Pineapple Juice
(unsweetened)

Harry of the
SAVOY
presents

**SAVOY HOTEL
COCKTAIL**

½ BOOTH'S GIN
¼ LILLET
¼ HERCULES
Stir well in ice, strain
into cocktail glass, and
squeeze lemon peel on
top.

its position was reinforced as the primary choice of liquor. One of the first films to showcase gin was *The Thin Man* (1934), starring William Powell and Myrna Loy as the witty, permanently tipsy Nick and Nora Charles, who sipped Dry Martinis and solved crimes, in that order. The costumes and sets were fabulous, and Nick and Nora's deluxe life was enviable. They were such crowd-pleasers that several sequels were released. Nora in particular was a modern character, a wise-cracking woman who knew how to work a cocktail shaker. This helped to increase sales of cocktail paraphernalia and recipe books to the point where home cocktail bars were soon essential installations across the USA.

In this era the Martini had a reputation as the drink of the erudite and the cosmopolitan. Mae West quipped in her film *Every Day's a Holiday* (1937) that she would be 'slipping out of wet clothes and into a Dry Martini'. Writer and performer Noel Coward opined that 'a perfect Martini should be made by filling a glass with gin, then waving it in the general direction of Italy' (where most of the world's vermouth came from). Film director Alfred Hitchcock joked that his Dry Martini should comprise 'one short glance at a bottle of vermouth'.

American pop culture in all its guises was greatly influential and was imitated around the world. Seeing beautiful and talented stars of screen, stage, music and literature enjoying gin was a priceless endorsement and reinforced its allure. King of Cool Frank Sinatra downed Martinis on

the Rocks, and Cole Porter wrote a song, 'Say It With Gin', for his musical *The New Yorkers*. *Casablanca*'s (1942) Ilsa, played by Ingrid Bergman, prompted Humphrey Bogart as bar-owner Rick to utter the immortal line: 'Of all the gin joints in all the towns in all the world, she walks into mine.' Who could forget the scene in the film *All About Eve* (1950) where Bette Davis drains her umpteenth Gibson (Dry Martini garnished with a pickled onion) and warns her guests to 'fasten your seatbelts, it's going to be a bumpy night'. Ernest Hemingway, that epitome of macho, was so enamoured of gin that his narrator in *A Farewell to Arms* rhapsodised about Martinis, claiming: 'I had never tasted anything so cool and clean. They made me feel civilized.' Debonair spies drank gin, too. James Bond, in the novels by Ian Fleming, imbibed Gin & Tonic, Pink Gin and Dry Martinis. In the book *Casino Royale* he instructed the barman on how to mix the Vesper, which included three parts of gin, one of vodka, vermouth and a thin slice of lemon peel. Shaken not stirred.

Gin was now up-to-the-minute and associated with success. Gordon's encouraged this prestige by paying blue-blooded, titled women to advertise the brand. The association with aristocracy was reinforced by the news that Britain's royal family were gin-drinking devotees and that the Gin & Dubonnet, Gin & Tonic and Dry Martini were particular favourites. America had gone wild for all things British in 1953, following the coronation of Queen

Elizabeth II, and distillers capitalised on the attention this generated.

But while gin was booming in America, in its birthplace the reputational rollercoaster was about to take another dip. Poor harvests during the 1930s led to a decline in the quality of gin. Premium spirits were reserved for export, for the sake of foreign currency earnings. Decent gin was in short supply during the Second World War, so smuggled goods or home-made distillates filled the void. The war transformed the public's outlook, behaviour and expectations. Austerity and rationing meant that post-war Britain was bleak. It was fast losing its empire as former colonies gained their independence, and its aura of invincibility was diminishing. Gin was no longer the progressive spirit of the 1920s and 1930s; the excitement and the sexiness had waned. The Bright Young Things were now the Tarnished Middle-Aged Things.

Gin became officially uncool on 6 October 1962, when the film *Dr. No* was released and viewers saw James Bond order a Martini made with vodka. This was a bellwether, because 007 was an icon and had a lifestyle that many aspired to. If the suave secret agent had eschewed gin, then they would, too. When the cultural revolution of the Swinging Sixties arrived, it was led by the youth who revelled in the summer of love, casual drug-use, sexual liberation and pleasure-seeking. Gin had no place in that social smorgasbord.

By that time vodka had become the contemporary drink and, because its flavour is so subtle, it was the perfect mixer. Its cleanliness and perceived purity were positive attributes, unlike highly aromatic gin, which was too perfumed, too fussy and too dated. The avant-garde chose vodka, and the gin industry could do nothing to persuade them otherwise.

G & T plus ice and a slice became a custom of the nou-veau riche, provincial golf-clubs and Beverly from *Abigail's Party*. At best, it was outmoded; at worst, it was naff.

Britain's declining position on the world stage coincided with the dwindling of gin's fortunes. The 1970s could be described as gin's Dark Ages, not only because the lights went out across swathes of the land due to lengthy black-outs and the three-day week, but because of civil strife and economic misery leading to the nation being described as 'the sick man of Europe'.

If you have not read the first chapter of this book, you may be weeping by now – but wipe away those tears, because in the late 1980s distillers spent millions to revive the fortunes of gin. Bombay Sapphire was launched and had a significant influence in changing people's attitudes to the venerable spirit. In its eye-catching, slick, blue glass bottle, Bombay Sapphire was a visual dog-whistle for the dashing, the chichi, the *soignées*.

Arguably the most considerable impact on gin's destiny was a change to a British law that stipulated that pot stills must hold at least 18 hectolitres of spirit (the equivalent of 2,572 standard-sized bottles). That rule favoured large established distilleries, but penalised start-ups. This status quo was successfully challenged by Sipsmith and Chase distilleries, and in 2009 legislation was enacted to permit the production of small batches of spirit. Boutique brands have flourished ever since.

Something about gin stimulates the imagination and liberates the can-do attitude in distillers, so what might previously have been considered unorthodox is now embraced for its ingenuity. Even producers in other sectors are not immune, with some brewers now distilling beer, cideries creating apple spirit, wine makers producing *aqua vitae* from grapes, and all of them releasing the distillates as gin, falling prey to the irresistible lure of juniper.

Across the globe, gin parlours, gin schools and gin dens are thriving with creativity, passion and enthusiasm. Gin has earned her position as the jewel in the crown and queen of the spirit world. Long may she reign.

THE COCKTAIL MENU

THESE RECIPES ARE for cocktails mentioned elsewhere in the book. Traditionally cocktails that contain fruit juice, cream, syrup and other thick-textured constituents should be shaken to ensure they are fully blended. Those that contain liquor only are normally stirred.

DRY MARTINI

Designed in the late nineteenth century, probably in the USA, the Dry Martini was partly responsible for gin becoming the most fashionable tipple for the decades between the two World Wars.

INGREDIENTS
50 ml gin
10 ml dry vermouth
Olive or lemon peel for a garnish

Method

Place a few cubes of ice into a cocktail shaker. Add the gin and vermouth. Let the ice chill the mixture, then stir it and strain into a glass. Garnish the rim with lemon peel, or place the olives onto a cocktail stick and dip into the liquid. A cocktail onion turns it into a Gibson. For an Extra Dry Martini, just rinse the glass in vermouth rather than mixing it with gin in the shaker.

James Bond, who imbibes Vodka Martinis in the films but Gin Martinis in the novels, always instructs the bartender that his cocktail should be 'shaken not stirred'. Shaking the Martini means that the ice cubes break into smaller pieces, melt quickly and dilute the ingredients. Some claim that this balances the flavours. Shaken or stirred is a personal preference.

Glassware

Martini glass or coupe chilled in the fridge.

———————

GIMLET

The Gimlet was imbibed by sailors on British naval ships in the nineteenth century because lime juice contains vitamin C, which prevents scurvy.

INGREDIENTS
50 ml Navy Strength Gin
50 ml lime cordial
Slice of lime

METHOD
Drop ice cubes into a cocktail shaker. Add the gin
and lime cordial and shake it. Strain into the glass
and garnish with a slice of lime.

GLASSWARE
Martini or coupe glass chilled in the fridge.

GIN & DUBONNET

This is a favourite of Queen Elizabeth II, who is said
to drink it as an aperitif. Dubonnet is a fortified wine
that contains bitter herbs and spices. It tastes similar
to red vermouth and was invented in France in 1864
as a tonic wine that included quinine to prevent
malaria.

INGREDIENTS
50 ml Dubonnet Rouge
25 ml gin
Lemon or orange peel

METHOD

Place a few cubes of ice into a cocktail shaker. Add the Dubonnet and gin. Let the ice chill the mixture, then stir and strain into a glass. Garnish the rim with lemon or orange peel.

GLASSWARE

Martini glass or coupe chilled in the fridge.

GIN & IT

The cocktail of the Roaring Twenties, especially among the Bright Young Things of London. It originated as a Sweet Martini in late nineteenth-century USA. 'It' refers to sweet Italian vermouth.

INGREDIENTS

50 ml gin
25 ml sweet vermouth
Maraschino cherries

METHOD

Pour the vermouth and gin directly into an Old Fashioned glass and stir it. Garnish with Maraschino cherries (one or three, never an even number). It is traditionally served without ice.

PINK GIN

Pink Gin was first consumed by sailors and passengers on British ships in the nineteenth century, as bitters were thought to prevent seasickness. This cocktail is not to be confused with a sweet modern gin category called Pink Gin, which, as the name suggests, is rose-hued due to the addition after distillation of fruits, flowers and vegetables such as rhubarb, rose, strawberry and raspberry, or their syrup equivalent. The recipe below is for the original nineteenth-century Pink Gin.

INGREDIENTS
50 ml Navy Strength Gin
2 dashes Angostura Bitters
Lemon peel

METHOD
Place a few cubes of ice into a cocktail shaker. Add the gin and bitters. Let the ice chill the mixture, then stir it and strain into a glass. Garnish the rim with lemon peel.

GLASSWARE
Martini glass or coupe chilled in the fridge.

VESPER MARTINI

This Martini was invented by novelist Ian Fleming and featured in the 1953 James Bond novel *Casino Royale*. It is named after Vesper Lynd, who was Bond's lover.

INGREDIENTS
60 ml London Dry Gin
20 ml vodka
10 ml dry vermouth
Lemon peel

METHOD
Place a few cubes of ice into a cocktail shaker. Add the gin, vodka and vermouth. Let the ice chill the mixture, then stir it and strain into a glass. Garnish the rim with lemon peel. As this is the James Bond Martini, the cocktail police will not mind if it is shaken, not stirred.

GLASSWARE
Martini glass or coupe chilled in the fridge.

DIFFERENT STYLES OF GIN AND JUNIPER SPIRITS

ALPINE Popular in Austria, Germany and Switzerland. Juniper is the dominant flavour, so the gin tastes pine-like and herbal.

BOROVIČKA Intensely resinous juniper-flavoured spirit widely consumed in the Czech Republic, Hungary and Slovakia. It is drunk chilled and neat.

GENEVER The Dutch spirit from which gin evolved. Also spelled jenever. Unlike gin, it is not used in cocktails; rather, it is drunk neat. It is made by combining a spirit that resembles whisky, comprised of mixed cereals, with a vodka-type spirit flavoured by juniper and other botanicals. The taste profile is malty compared to that of gin.

GIN DE MENORCA, AKA GIN DE MAHÓN This gin has protected geographical indication status and can only call itself Gin de Menorca if it is distilled on the eponymous

Spanish Balearic island. Mahon, capital of Menorca, was a British naval base in the early eighteenth century, and a gin distillery was later established there to serve passing ships and land-based officials.

HOLLANDS A spirit closely related to genever, but with fewer botanicals, sometimes only juniper. Its hey day was the eighteenth and nineteenth centuries, but several twenty-first-century distilleries have revived the style.

LONDON DRY The world's most popular type of gin. London Dry is a manufacturing technique, and the gin can be made anywhere, not just in London. It is created by redistilling alcohol and natural botanicals (primarily juniper) that aromatise and flavour the spirit during distillation, and not after. No artificial ingredients may be used, and the only extra substance that may be added is water, to dilute it before bottling.

NAVY STRENGTH Any gin can be defined thus because the name signifies only the amount of alcohol. In the centuries when spirits were routinely carried on board British naval ships, the Navy required distillers to supply gin and rum at high ABVs. To ensure that the spirit was the strength the producer claimed, and the Navy was not being swindled, the ship's pursers (pussars in naval lingo) tested it by dousing a tiny amount of gunpowder in gin (or rum) and lighting it. If the gunpowder ignited, then the spirit was at least 100 per cent proof, or 57 per cent ABV.

OLD TOM Old Tom is sweeter than London Dry. It originated in eighteenth-century Britain, when gin needed to be sweetened to make it palatable. When London Dry was introduced in the nineteenth century, Old Tom went out of fashion, but today it has been restored as part of the gin renaissance, and distilleries produce it worldwide.

PLYMOUTH GIN Similar to London Dry, but fruitier, with a more delicate juniper character. It originated in 1793 at the Blackfriar's Distillery in the British port city of Plymouth, which was conveniently located to supply British naval ships.

SLOE GIN Technically a liqueur due to the amount of sugar added, sloe gin is simple to make. Pick sloes from a hedgerow (or buy online) and freeze them to break the skins. Place the sloes in a large glass jar and add sugar. Pour quality gin over the fruit. The ratio of gin to fruit and sugar is 1 litre of spirit, 500 g sloes and 250 g white sugar. Close the jar and shake vigorously. Store in a dark cupboard and shake the jar every day for a week to dissolve the sugar. After that, shake it every week for three months. Strain the liquid into a bottle. It is now ready to drink on its own, with tonic or with sparkling wine.

STEINHÄGER A German style of gin, flavoured only with juniper and in production since the eighteenth century in Steinhagen, North Rhine-Westphalia.

WACHOLDER A juniper-flavoured distillate hailing from Germany's Westphalia, Rhineland, Lippe and Emsland regions. Wacholder is the German word for juniper and denotes any juniper spirit including genever and gin. It is drunk in shots, often as a chaser to beer.

TIPS FOR THE PERFECT G & T

With just three components, Gin & Tonic is one of the easiest cocktails to make, but that simplicity also means that it is one of the easiest to spoil.

The ingredients are:
50 ml gin (any style)
Tonic water
Garnish.

The order in which it is concocted is important. Chill the glass, add the ice cubes, pour in the gin, then add the tonic. Stir the mix before adding the garnish.

For the perfect G & T, follow these instructions.

☞ Choose a glass with a wide circumference to enhance the fragrant botanicals in the gin. Suitable glasses are Bordeaux red wine, *copa de balon*, or tumbler. It should be chilled beforehand.

☞ Ice: use plenty of large cubes! A full glass of ice will not dilute the cocktail.

☞ Ratio of gin to tonic: 25 per cent gin and 75 per cent tonic is recommended, but it is a personal decision as to how much or how little to add.

☞ Tonic water: this accounts for the majority of the cocktail, so ensure it is first-rate and crafted with real botanicals, not flavourings, so that it will complement the gin.

☞ Garnish: check the dominant flavour profile of the gin and match a garnish accordingly. For instance, if it is floral, then select a herb or a flower; for spicy, choose black peppercorns or a stick of cinnamon; for citrus, go for orange or grapefruit peel, or a wedge of lime.

G & T APERITIF

A Gin & Tonic before a meal is the perfect aperitif, and your digestive system will thank you. Juniper contains compounds that stimulate enzymes. This, in turn, increases the flow of bile which is critical in digestion and assists the absorption of nutrients into the bloodstream. Juniper can also alleviate heartburn. Premium tonic water contains Cinchona bark, which promotes the release of digestive juices and is used to treat bloating.

FURTHER READING

Richard Barnett, *The Book of Gin* (Grove Press, 2011)

David T. Smith, *The Gin Dictionary* (Mitchell Beazley, 2018)

Jessica Warner, *Craze* (Random House, 2003)

Olivia Williams, *Gin Glorious Gin* (Headline, 2014)

LIST OF ILLUSTRATIONS

Analytical, as Applied to the Arts and Manufacturers,
Philadelphia, 1877. (Photo: Courtesy of Science History
Institute)

p. 62 1934 advert for Gordon's Gin, from *The Sketch*. (Hiu.
Ld.52 [1934])

p. 64 'A Midnight Modern Conversation', print by Ernst
Ludwig Creite after William Hogarth. (Rijksmuseum,
Amsterdam)

p. 65 Punch bowl depicting Bonnie Prince Charlie. (British
Museum, London)

p. 67 1939 advertisement for Pimm's No. 1, from *Punch*.
(C.194.b.199)

p. 72 Jerry Thomas. From Jerry Thomas, *How to Mix Drinks,
or, The Bon-Vivant's Companion*, New York, 1862.
(7945.bb.16)

p. 75 'Stop when you see this sign', the insignia plate the
Bureau of Prohibition adopted for use by prohibition
agents when stopping suspected automobiles. (Photo:
Library of Congress)

p. 76 Woman pouring alcohol into a cup from a cane during
Prohibition, 1922. (Photo: Library of Congress)

p. 80 British bartenders and their cocktails, from *An Anthology
of Cocktails*, Booth's Distilleries, *c*. 1930. (W8/4136)

p. 82 Poster for *The Thin Man*, 1934. (Photo: Heritage
Auctions)

p. 84 Ian Fleming, *Casino Royale*, London, 1957. Front cover
design. (Adrian Harrington Rare Books)

Also available in this series

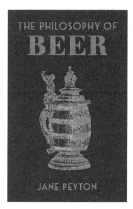

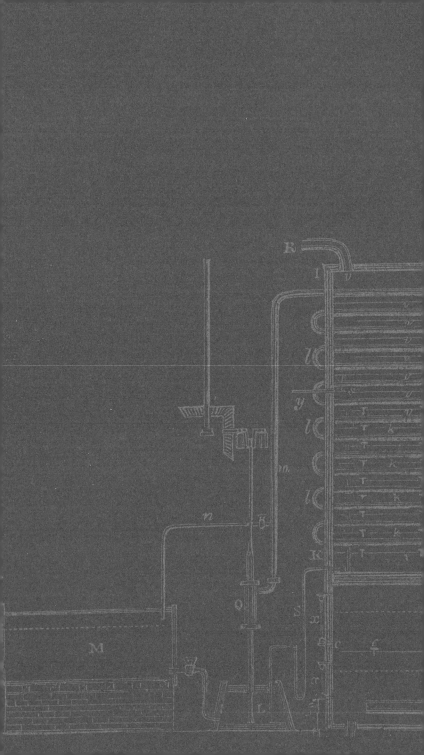